# THE CODE OF HAMMURABI

*Unveiling the Ancient Principles of Justice Through Modern Insights*

By

ELIJAH UR

Copyright © 2024 by ELIJAH UR

All rights reserved. No part of this publication may be reproduced, stored or
transmitted in any form or by any means, electronic, mechanical,
photocopying, recording, scanning, or otherwise without written permission
from the publisher. It is illegal to copy this book, post it to a website, or
distribute it by any other means without permission.

First edition

**THE CODE OF HAMMURABI**

# TABLE OF CONTENTS

## 1
### INTRODUCTION:
Setting the Stage for Hammurabi's Code
- The Rise of Babylon: A Flourishing Civilization
- Hammurabi's Reign: A Time of Innovation and Legal Development

## 2
### DECIPHERING THE CODE:
Unraveling the Legal Framework
- Structure and Composition of Hammurabi's Code
- Key Legal Principles and Their Application

## 3
### JUSTICE IN ANCIENT BABYLON:
Exploring the Legal System
- Institutions of Justice: Courts, Judges, and Officials
- Legal Procedures and Practices in Ancient Babylon

## 4
### MODERN INSIGHTS ON ANCIENT JUSTICE:
Bridging the Gap
- Comparative Analysis: Hammurabi's Code and Contemporary Legal Systems
- Relevance and Applications of Ancient Legal Principles Today

## 5
### DISCOVERIES AND INTERPRETATIONS:
Insights from Archaeology
- Archaeological Uncoverings: Texts, Tablets, and Artifacts

**THE CODE OF HAMMURABI**

Challenges and Strategies in Interpreting Ancient Legal Texts Today

## 6
## LEGACY AND INFLUENCE:
## Hammurabi's Code in History

Impact on Subsequent Legal Systems: Tracing the Influence

Lessons Learned and Applied from Hammurabi's Code

## 7
## CASE STUDIES AND PRACTICAL APPLICATIONS:
## Learning from History

Real-Life Examples: Applying Ancient Legal Principles

Contemporary Relevance: Insights for Legal Practice Today

## 8
## DEBATES AND DISCOURSES:
## Critiques and Controversies

Ethical Considerations: Examining the Moral Implications

Interpretation Challenges and Debates Among Scholars

## 9
## CONCLUSION:
## Reflections and Future Directions

Understanding Ancient Principles of Justice: A Journey's End

Looking Ahead: Future Research and Implications for Legal Scholarship

**THE CODE OF HAMMURABI**

# 1

# INTRODUCTION:

# Setting the Stage for Hammurabi's Code

In the ancient land of Mesopotamia, amidst the bustling city-state of Babylon, a pivotal moment in legal history unfolded. Babylon, with its strategic location and thriving economy, emerged as a cultural and political powerhouse in the ancient Near East. At its helm stood Hammurabi, a visionary ruler whose reign marked a period of unprecedented innovation and legal development.

## *The Rise of Babylon: A Flourishing Civilization*

Babylon's ascent to prominence was fueled by its strategic location along the Euphrates River, which facilitated trade and cultural exchange with neighboring regions. As Babylon grew into a bustling metropolis, it became a melting pot of diverse peoples and cultures, fostering a spirit of cosmopolitanism and intellectual inquiry. The city's wealth and influence extended far beyond its borders, attracting merchants, artisans, and scholars from across the region.

Under Hammurabi's rule, Babylon experienced a golden age of prosperity and growth. Hammurabi, hailed as a wise and just ruler, embarked on ambitious initiatives to centralize authority and promote economic development. His reign saw the construction of grand architectural projects, such as ziggurats and temples, which served as symbols of Babylonian power and prestige.

**THE CODE OF HAMMURABI**

## *Hammurabi's Reign: A Time of Innovation and Legal Development*

Central to Hammurabi's vision for Babylon was the establishment of a comprehensive legal code that would govern every aspect of society. Hammurabi recognized the importance of codifying laws to ensure justice and order within his realm. Thus, he embarked on the monumental task of compiling a set of laws that would address a wide range of legal issues, from criminal offenses to commercial transactions.

Hammurabi's Code, engraved onto a stele and displayed prominently in public spaces, represented a groundbreaking achievement in legal history. It provided a framework for resolving disputes, maintaining order, and ensuring the equitable treatment of all subjects under Hammurabi's rule. The code covered a wide range of subjects, including criminal law, civil law, family law, and commercial law, reflecting the diverse needs of Babylonian society.

**THE CODE OF HAMMURABI**

However, Hammurabi's legal innovations were not without controversy. While his code represented a significant step towards the codification of laws, it also reflected the biases and inequalities of ancient Babylonian society. Critics argue that certain provisions of Hammurabi's Code, such as the lex talionis principle of "an eye for an eye," were harsh and disproportionate by modern standards.

# 2

# DECIPHERING THE CODE:

## Unraveling the Legal Framework

Hammurabi's Code stands as one of the most significant legal documents from ancient Mesopotamia, offering invaluable insights into the legal framework of Babylonian society during the reign of King Hammurabi in the 18th century BCE. Deciphering this code is akin to unraveling the complexities of a bygone era, where laws were not merely sets of rules but reflections of societal values, power dynamics, and the king's authority.

## Structure and Composition of Hammurabi's Code

The structure and composition of Hammurabi's Code provide a window into the organization and governance of Babylonian society. Unlike modern legal codes, which are often arranged thematically or by subject matter, Hammurabi's Code follows a more hierarchical structure, with the laws arranged according to a system of justice based on retributive justice, also known as lex talionis or "an eye for an eye."

The code consists of a prologue and an epilogue, framing the laws within the divine authority of the gods and the king's role as the dispenser of justice. Within these bookends lies a collection of nearly 300 laws, inscribed on a stela of black diorite and displayed in public for all to see. Each law is preceded by a casuistic statement, outlining a specific scenario or offense, followed by the prescribed punishment or remedy.

The hierarchical nature of the code is evident in its organization, with laws pertaining to different social classes and legal statuses arranged in distinct sections. For example, laws related to property rights, contracts, and commercial transactions are grouped together, reflecting the importance of commerce and trade in Babylonian society. Similarly, laws governing familial relations, marriage, and inheritance are given prominence, underscoring the significance of kinship ties and social order.

## *Key Legal Principles and Their Application*

Embedded within the text of Hammurabi's Code are a multitude of legal principles that offer valuable insights into the Babylonian legal system and its underlying ethos. One of the most prominent principles is that of strict liability, where individuals are held accountable for their actions regardless of intent or negligence. This principle is exemplified in laws governing property damage, personal injury, and contractual obligations, where the perpetrator is required to compensate the victim or suffer a commensurate punishment.

Another key legal principle embodied in Hammurabi's Code is that of proportionate justice, whereby punishments are calibrated to fit the severity of the offense. This principle is encapsulated in the famous lex talionis provision, which stipulates that the punishment should be equivalent to the harm caused. For example, if a person injures another by striking them, the perpetrator shall receive a similar injury in return.

Moreover, the code reflects the concept of social stratification and differential treatment based on social status. While the laws strive for impartiality and equality before the law, there are instances where certain classes of individuals, such as nobles or slaves, are subject to different standards of justice. This hierarchical approach to law enforcement underscores the hierarchical nature of Babylonian society, where social status and privilege conferred certain rights and privileges.

Critically examining the key legal principles and their application in Hammurabi's Code reveals both the strengths and limitations of the Babylonian legal system. While the code provided a degree of legal certainty and predictability, its reliance on strict, punitive measures also raised questions about fairness, equity, and access to justice. Moreover, the hierarchical nature of the code perpetuated social inequalities and reinforced existing power structures, highlighting the inherent tensions between law and justice in ancient Mesopotamia.

# 3

# JUSTICE IN ANCIENT BABYLON:

# Exploring the Legal System

Ancient Babylonian society was structured around a complex legal system that sought to maintain social order, resolve disputes, and uphold the authority of the king. Exploring the intricacies of this legal system provides valuable insights into the mechanisms of justice in one of the world's earliest civilizations.

## *Institutions of Justice: Courts, Judges, and Officials*

The administration of justice in ancient Babylon was overseen by a network of institutions, including courts, judges, and legal officials. At the heart of the legal system was the king, who served as the ultimate arbiter of justice and the embodiment of divine authority. Underneath the king were a hierarchy of judges and officials responsible for interpreting and applying the law.

Courts in ancient Babylon were typically decentralized, with disputes adjudicated at the local level by magistrates or elders appointed by the king. These local courts were responsible for hearing a wide range of cases, including civil disputes, criminal offenses, and matters of family law. In more serious or complex cases, appeals could be made to higher courts or directly to the king himself.

Judges in ancient Babylon were expected to possess a thorough knowledge of the law and a keen understanding of legal procedures. They were tasked with presiding over court proceedings, weighing evidence, and rendering impartial judgments. Judges were often drawn from the ranks of the priesthood or the nobility, reflecting the close ties between religion, politics, and law in Babylonian society.

**THE CODE OF HAMMURABI**

Legal officials played a crucial role in the administration of justice, assisting judges in their duties and ensuring the smooth functioning of the legal system. These officials included scribes, who recorded court proceedings and maintained legal records, as well as bailiffs, who enforced court orders and carried out punishments. Together, these institutions formed the backbone of the Babylonian legal system, providing a framework for the resolution of disputes and the dispensation of justice.

## *Legal Procedures and Practices in Ancient Babylon*

Legal procedures in ancient Babylon were governed by a set of established practices and protocols designed to ensure fairness, transparency, and due process. Central to these procedures was the concept of oral testimony, where parties to a dispute presented their arguments and evidence before a judge or panel of judges.

The legal process typically began with the filing of a complaint or petition by the plaintiff, who sought redress for a perceived wrong or injury. The defendant was then summoned to appear before the court to respond to the allegations and present their defense. Both parties were given the opportunity to call witnesses, present evidence, and make arguments in support of their case.

Once all relevant evidence had been heard and considered, the judge rendered a decision based on the merits of the case and the applicable law. Judgments were often delivered orally, with the reasoning behind the decision explained to the parties involved. In cases where the judgment was contested or appealed, the matter could be referred to a higher court or to the king for final resolution.

Legal proceedings in ancient Babylon were characterized by a strong emphasis on mediation and conciliation, with judges playing an active role in facilitating negotiations between the parties. Alternative dispute resolution mechanisms, such as arbitration and mediation, were commonly employed to resolve conflicts and avoid lengthy court battles.

However, despite the presence of formal legal procedures and institutions, the administration of justice in ancient Babylon was not without its flaws and limitations. The legal system was subject to the biases and prejudices of those who administered it, and there were instances of corruption, favoritism, and abuse of power. Moreover, access to justice was often uneven, with different social classes and groups afforded varying degrees of protection under the law.

# 4

# MODERN INSIGHTS ON ANCIENT JUSTICE:

## Bridging the Gap

The study of ancient justice systems, such as Hammurabi's Code, offers more than just historical curiosity; it provides modern scholars and legal practitioners with valuable insights into the evolution of legal thought and the enduring principles of justice. By conducting a comparative analysis between Hammurabi's Code and contemporary legal systems, as well as examining the relevance and applications of ancient legal principles today, we can bridge the gap between the past and the present, enriching our understanding of law and justice in both contexts.

## *Comparative Analysis: Hammurabi's Code and Contemporary Legal Systems*

Conducting a comparative analysis between Hammurabi's Code and contemporary legal systems allows us to identify similarities, differences, and enduring themes in the administration of justice across time and space. Despite the vast temporal and cultural divide separating ancient Babylon from the modern world, there are striking parallels in the legal principles and practices employed by Hammurabi and contemporary legal systems.

One of the most salient similarities between Hammurabi's Code and modern legal systems is the emphasis on codified law as a means of regulating social behavior and resolving disputes. Both systems rely on written laws and legal codes to provide a framework for adjudicating conflicts and maintaining order within society. However, while modern legal codes are often more comprehensive and complex than Hammurabi's

Code, they share a common purpose: to establish norms, define rights and responsibilities, and ensure the fair and equitable treatment of individuals before the law.

Moreover, both Hammurabi's Code and contemporary legal systems exhibit a commitment to the principles of justice, fairness, and equity. While the specific manifestations of these principles may vary across time and culture, the underlying values remain consistent. For example, the concept of proportionate justice, embodied in Hammurabi's lex talionis provision, finds echoes in modern legal principles of proportionality and just punishment.

However, despite these similarities, there are also significant differences between Hammurabi's Code and contemporary legal systems, reflecting the evolution of legal thought and practice over millennia. One notable difference is the role of religion and divine authority in ancient Babylonian law, where the king served as both the temporal and spiritual leader of society. In contrast, modern legal systems are typically secular in nature, with a separation of church and state and a focus on the rule of law as the ultimate authority.

Moreover, while Hammurabi's Code was a product of its time and place, shaped by the cultural, social, and political context of ancient Babylon, contemporary legal systems are influenced by a diverse array of factors, including globalization, technological advancement, and evolving social norms. This dynamic and adaptive nature of modern legal systems reflects the complexities of modern society and the need for flexible and responsive legal frameworks.

## *Relevance and Applications of Ancient Legal Principles Today*

Despite the temporal and cultural distance separating ancient Babylon from the modern world, the legal principles embodied in Hammurabi's Code remain relevant and applicable today. The enduring themes of justice, fairness, and equity resonate across time and culture, providing a foundation for contemporary legal thought and practice.

One area where ancient legal principles continue to inform modern legal systems is in the realm of criminal law and punishment. The concept of proportionate justice, exemplified in Hammurabi's lex talionis provision, continues to shape contemporary notions of just punishment and the principles of retribution, deterrence, and rehabilitation. Moreover, the emphasis on due process and the fair treatment of defendants reflects a fundamental commitment to the principles of justice and human rights.

Another area where ancient legal principles find contemporary relevance is in the realm of contract law and commercial transactions. The emphasis on contractual obligations and the enforcement of agreements reflects a recognition of the importance of economic exchange and the need for legal certainty and predictability in commercial dealings. Moreover, the principles of good faith and fair dealing, embodied in

Hammurabi's Code, continue to underpin modern contract law and business ethics.

Furthermore, the emphasis on mediation and conciliation in ancient Babylonian law provides valuable lessons for modern approaches to dispute resolution and conflict management. Alternative dispute resolution mechanisms, such as arbitration and mediation, offer parties a more flexible and collaborative means of resolving conflicts outside of the formal legal system, promoting efficiency, cost-effectiveness, and greater satisfaction with the outcome.

# 5

# DISCOVERIES AND INTERPRETATIONS:

## Insights from Archaeology

Archaeology plays a crucial role in uncovering and interpreting the remnants of ancient civilizations, offering valuable insights into their cultures, societies, and legal systems. In the case of Hammurabi's Code and ancient Babylonian law, archaeological discoveries provide a wealth of primary sources, including texts, tablets, and artifacts, that shed light on the legal practices and norms of the time. Additionally, archaeologists face numerous challenges in interpreting ancient legal texts today, requiring careful analysis and consideration of contextual factors to reconstruct the legal landscape of ancient Mesopotamia.

## *Archaeological Uncoverings: Texts, Tablets, and Artifacts*

Archaeological excavations in Mesopotamia have yielded a treasure trove of textual and material evidence related to ancient Babylonian law. Among the most significant discoveries are the clay tablets containing fragments of Hammurabi's Code and other legal documents, such as contracts, decrees, and administrative records. These tablets, inscribed in cuneiform script, provide firsthand accounts of legal transactions, disputes, and judgments, offering invaluable insights into the legal framework and practices of ancient Babylonian society.

In addition to textual evidence, archaeologists have unearthed a variety of artifacts that offer glimpses into the daily lives and legal practices of the ancient Babylonians. These artifacts include seals, seal impressions, and other administrative tools used in the documentation and enforcement of legal agreements. For example, cylinder seals bearing the names and titles of individuals served as personal signatures, while seal impressions stamped onto clay tablets authenticated legal transactions and contracts.

Moreover, architectural remains, such as temples, palaces, and administrative buildings, provide clues about the spatial organization and functioning of the legal system in ancient Babylon. For instance, the discovery of courtroom structures and archives within administrative complexes suggests the presence of formal legal institutions and procedures for adjudicating disputes and administering justice.

Overall, the archaeological evidence related to ancient Babylonian law offers a multidimensional view of the legal system, encompassing both textual and material culture. By piecing together these fragments of the past, archaeologists and historians can reconstruct the legal landscape of ancient Mesopotamia and gain a deeper understanding of the principles and practices that governed Babylonian society.

**THE CODE OF HAMMURABI**

## *Challenges and Strategies in Interpreting Ancient Legal Texts Today*

Interpreting ancient legal texts poses numerous challenges for modern scholars, requiring careful analysis and contextualization to decipher their meaning and significance. One of the primary challenges is the preservation and decipherment of cuneiform script, which requires specialized expertise and training to read and interpret accurately. Moreover, the fragmentary nature of many ancient texts presents additional obstacles, as scholars must piece together disparate fragments and reconstruct missing portions to make sense of the whole.

Furthermore, the language and terminology used in ancient legal texts may be unfamiliar or ambiguous to modern readers, requiring linguistic and philological expertise to decipher and translate. Legal terminology, in particular, may vary in meaning and usage across different contexts and time periods, complicating efforts to accurately interpret ancient legal documents.

**THE CODE OF HAMMURABI**

Additionally, the cultural and historical context in which ancient legal texts were produced must be taken into account when interpreting their meaning and significance. Social, political, and religious factors may influence the content and interpretation of legal texts, necessitating a nuanced understanding of the cultural milieu in which they were written.

To address these challenges, scholars employ a variety of strategies and methodologies, including comparative analysis, linguistic analysis, and contextual interpretation. By comparing similar texts from different time periods or regions, scholars can identify recurring themes, patterns, and legal norms that provide insights into broader legal principles and practices.

Moreover, interdisciplinary approaches, such as archaeology, history, and anthropology, allow scholars to contextualize legal texts within the broader social, political, and economic dynamics of ancient societies. By examining material culture, architectural remains, and other archaeological evidence alongside textual sources, scholars can reconstruct the lived experiences of individuals within legal systems and institutions.

**THE CODE OF HAMMURABI**

# 6

# LEGACY AND INFLUENCE:

## Hammurabi's Code in History

Hammurabi's Code, one of the earliest known legal codes in human history, has left an indelible mark on subsequent legal systems and continues to shape our understanding of law and justice. Tracing the legacy and influence of Hammurabi's Code reveals its enduring impact on the development of legal thought and practice across cultures and time periods. Moreover, the lessons learned and applied from Hammurabi's Code offer valuable insights into the principles and values that underpin the administration of justice in societies past and present.

## *Impact on Subsequent Legal Systems: Tracing the Influence*

The influence of Hammurabi's Code can be observed in the development of legal systems and traditions across the ancient Near East and beyond. From the Code of Ur-Nammu in Sumer to the Mosaic Law in ancient Israel, echoes of Hammurabi's legal principles and practices reverberate throughout the ancient world. One of the most significant legacies of Hammurabi's Code is its codification of laws and its establishment of a written legal code as the foundation of legal governance.

Moreover, the concept of lex talionis, or "an eye for an eye," embodied in Hammurabi's Code, has been cited as a foundational principle in numerous legal traditions, including ancient Greek and Roman law. While the literal application of this principle may have fallen out of favor in modern legal systems, its underlying ethos of proportionate justice continues to inform contemporary notions of just punishment and the principles of retribution and deterrence.

Furthermore, Hammurabi's Code exerted a profound influence on the development of Islamic law, particularly in the areas of criminal law and family law. The Qur'anic concept of qisas, or retaliatory justice, bears striking similarities to the lex talionis principle found in Hammurabi's Code, reflecting the enduring resonance of ancient legal norms in shaping the legal landscape of the Islamic world.

In addition to its direct influence on subsequent legal systems, Hammurabi's Code has also served as a source of inspiration and emulation for later generations of lawmakers and jurists. The recognition of written law as a tool for governance and the emphasis on fairness, equity, and accountability embodied in Hammurabi's Code continue to resonate with modern legal scholars and practitioners seeking to uphold the rule of law and promote justice in society.

## *Lessons Learned and Applied from Hammurabi's Code*

The enduring legacy of Hammurabi's Code offers valuable lessons for contemporary legal systems and practitioners seeking to navigate the complexities of law and justice in the modern world. One such lesson is the importance of codified law as a means of ensuring legal certainty, predictability, and transparency. By establishing a written legal code, Hammurabi sought to provide a framework for adjudicating disputes and maintaining order within society, a principle that remains relevant in contemporary legal systems.

Moreover, the emphasis on proportionate justice and the equitable treatment of individuals before the law, embodied in Hammurabi's Code, highlights the fundamental values that underpin the administration of justice in societies past and present. By striving to uphold these principles, modern legal systems can promote fairness, equity, and accountability in the application of the law, thereby fostering public trust and confidence in the legal system.

Furthermore, the legacy of Hammurabi's Code serves as a reminder of the enduring power of law as a tool for governance and social cohesion. By enshrining legal norms and principles in written form, societies can establish a foundation for stability, order, and justice, even in the face of political upheaval and social change.

# 7

# CASE STUDIES AND PRACTICAL APPLICATIONS:

## Learning from History

Examining real-life examples and practical applications of ancient legal principles offers valuable insights into the relevance and applicability of historical legal systems to contemporary legal practice. By analyzing case studies and drawing lessons from history, we can glean valuable lessons for navigating the complexities of law and justice in the modern world, while also shedding light on the enduring relevance of ancient legal norms and principles.

## *Real-Life Examples: Applying Ancient Legal Principles*

One of the most compelling ways to understand the practical applications of ancient legal principles is through the analysis of real-life case studies. By examining specific legal disputes and their resolution within the framework of ancient legal systems, we can gain a deeper understanding of the principles and practices that governed everyday life in ancient societies.

For example, the case of the stolen ox, as outlined in Hammurabi's Code, provides a poignant illustration of the principles of restitution and retribution in ancient Babylonian law. According to the code, if a man's ox was stolen and subsequently recovered, the thief was required to pay double the value of the stolen ox as compensation. This principle of double restitution reflects the Babylonian emphasis on restoring the victim to their original state and ensuring that justice is served.

THE CODE OF HAMMURABI

Similarly, the case of marital infidelity, as addressed in the Code of Ur-Nammu, offers insights into the regulation of personal conduct and familial relations in ancient Sumerian society. According to the code, if a man's wife was accused of infidelity and found guilty, she and her lover were to be bound together and thrown into the water, a form of punishment known as the ordeal by water. This harsh penalty underscores the seriousness with which marital fidelity was viewed in ancient Sumerian culture and the lengths to which authorities would go to maintain social order and moral integrity.

By analyzing these and other real-life examples from ancient legal systems, modern scholars and legal practitioners can gain valuable insights into the principles and practices that governed justice in antiquity. Moreover, these case studies serve as cautionary tales, highlighting the pitfalls and limitations of applying ancient legal norms and principles to contemporary contexts without due consideration for cultural, social, and historical differences.

**THE CODE OF HAMMURABI**

## Contemporary Relevance: Insights for Legal Practice Today

Despite the temporal and cultural differences separating ancient legal systems from modern legal practice, there are valuable insights to be gleaned from the study of historical legal norms and principles. By drawing parallels between ancient and contemporary legal systems, we can identify enduring themes and values that continue to shape the administration of justice in the modern world.

For example, the emphasis on fairness, equity, and accountability embodied in Hammurabi's Code and other ancient legal texts resonates with contemporary notions of procedural justice and the rule of law. By upholding these principles, modern legal systems can promote public trust and confidence in the fairness and impartiality of the legal process.

Moreover, the emphasis on alternative dispute resolution mechanisms, such as mediation and arbitration, in ancient legal systems offers valuable lessons for addressing the challenges of modern litigation. By providing parties with a forum for resolving conflicts outside of the formal legal system, alternative dispute resolution mechanisms can promote efficiency, cost-effectiveness, and greater satisfaction with the outcome.

Furthermore, the recognition of written law as a tool for governance and social cohesion, as exemplified in Hammurabi's Code and other ancient legal codes, underscores the importance of legal certainty and predictability in maintaining order within society. By establishing clear and transparent legal norms and procedures, modern legal systems can provide a framework for resolving disputes and adjudicating conflicts in a fair and equitable manner.

# 8

# DEBATES AND DISCOURSES:

# Critiques and Controversies

The study of ancient legal systems, such as Hammurabi's Code, is not without its critiques and controversies. Ethical considerations and interpretation challenges abound, sparking debates among scholars and practitioners alike. By critically examining these debates and discourses, we can gain a deeper understanding of the moral implications and interpretation challenges inherent in the study of ancient legal texts.

## *Ethical Considerations: Examining the Moral Implications*

One of the central ethical considerations in the study of Hammurabi's Code and other ancient legal systems is the question of justice and morality. Critics argue that some of the laws and practices codified in ancient legal texts, including Hammurabi's Code, are morally objectionable by contemporary standards. For example, the lex talionis provision, which mandates "an eye for an eye" and "a tooth for a tooth," is often cited as an example of primitive and barbaric justice, incompatible with modern notions of human rights and dignity.

Moreover, the treatment of certain social groups, such as slaves, women, and foreigners, in ancient legal systems has been the subject of ethical scrutiny. Critics argue that the unequal treatment and marginalization of these groups reflect the biases and prejudices of ancient societies, perpetuating systems of oppression and exploitation.

Furthermore, the use of harsh and disproportionate punishments, such as corporal and capital punishment, raises ethical questions about the efficacy and morality of retributive justice. Critics argue that punitive measures, such as mutilation and execution, are inherently cruel and dehumanizing, violating the principles of human dignity and respect for life.

However, defenders of ancient legal systems counter these critiques by contextualizing the laws and practices within the social, cultural, and historical milieu in which they were produced. They argue that ancient legal codes, such as Hammurabi's Code, served as a means of maintaining social order and stability in the absence of modern institutions of governance and law enforcement. Moreover, they contend that the lex talionis principle and other punitive measures were intended to deter wrongdoing and promote accountability, rather than exacting arbitrary vengeance.

In addition to ethical considerations surrounding justice and morality, the study of ancient legal systems also raises questions about cultural relativism and the universality of legal norms. Critics argue that imposing modern ethical standards and values on ancient societies risks imposing anachronistic judgments and obscuring the unique cultural contexts in which these legal systems operated. Moreover, they contend that ethical judgments should be tempered by an appreciation for the diversity of human experience and the complexities of historical and cultural context.

## *Interpretation Challenges and Debates Among Scholars*

Interpreting ancient legal texts presents numerous challenges and debates among scholars, ranging from linguistic and philological issues to broader questions of historical context and cultural interpretation. One of the primary challenges is the preservation and decipherment of cuneiform script, which requires specialized expertise and training to read and interpret accurately. Moreover, the fragmentary nature of many ancient texts poses additional obstacles, as scholars must reconstruct missing portions and decipher obscure or ambiguous passages to make sense of the whole.

Furthermore, the interpretation of legal terminology and concepts in ancient texts can be fraught with ambiguity and complexity. Words and phrases that appear straightforward may carry nuanced meanings and connotations that vary across different contexts and time periods. Moreover, legal terminology may evolve over time, complicating efforts to accurately interpret ancient legal texts within their historical and cultural context.

Moreover, debates among scholars often revolve around the broader question of how to interpret and contextualize ancient legal texts within the social, political, and cultural dynamics of their time. Some scholars advocate for a strict textualist approach, focusing exclusively on the literal meaning of the words and phrases contained within the legal texts. Others adopt a more contextualist approach, considering the broader historical and cultural context in which the texts were produced and seeking to understand the underlying principles and values that informed legal decision-making.

**THE CODE OF HAMMURABI**

# 9

# CONCLUSION:

# Reflections and Future Directions

As we conclude our journey through the exploration of ancient legal systems, particularly focusing on Hammurabi's Code, it is essential to reflect on the insights gained and consider future directions for research and scholarship in the field of legal history and comparative law. Understanding ancient principles of justice offers profound insights into the foundations of legal thought and practice, while also providing valuable lessons for navigating the complexities of law and justice in the modern world. Looking ahead, future research holds the potential to deepen our understanding of ancient legal systems and their implications for contemporary legal scholarship and practice.

## *Understanding Ancient Principles of Justice: A Journey's End*

Our journey through the study of ancient legal systems has been both enlightening and challenging, as we grappled with the complexities of deciphering ancient texts, interpreting legal principles, and navigating ethical considerations. Through our exploration of Hammurabi's Code and other ancient legal codes, we have gained a deeper appreciation for the enduring significance of legal norms and principles in shaping human society and governance.

One of the key takeaways from our study is the recognition of the universality of certain legal principles and values, such as fairness, equity, and accountability. Despite the vast temporal and cultural divide separating ancient legal systems from modern legal practice, we have observed striking parallels in the principles and practices that govern justice and law enforcement. By

**THE CODE OF HAMMURABI**

tracing the evolution of legal thought and practice across time and culture, we have gained valuable insights into the enduring nature of human concerns and aspirations for justice and order.

Moreover, our journey has underscored the importance of contextualizing ancient legal texts within their historical, cultural, and social context. By understanding the broader dynamics of ancient societies, including their political structures, religious beliefs, and social norms, we can gain a deeper understanding of the motivations and intentions behind the laws and practices codified in ancient legal codes. This contextualization allows us to appreciate the complexities of legal decision-making in ancient times and avoid imposing anachronistic judgments on past societies.

In conclusion, our journey through the study of ancient legal systems has provided us with a rich tapestry of insights into the foundations of legal thought and practice. By engaging with the principles and practices embodied in Hammurabi's Code and other ancient legal codes, we have gained a deeper understanding of the enduring significance of legal norms and principles in shaping human societies past and present.

## *Looking Ahead: Future Research and Implications for Legal Scholarship*

As we look to the future, there are numerous avenues for further research and exploration in the field of ancient legal history and comparative law. One promising area of inquiry is the comparative analysis of ancient legal systems, exploring the similarities and differences between different legal traditions and their implications for the development of legal thought and practice. By examining cross-cultural influences and exchanges, scholars can gain a more nuanced understanding of the dynamics of legal evolution and transmission across time and space.

Moreover, future research holds the potential to deepen our understanding of specific aspects of ancient legal systems, such as the role of legal institutions, the administration of justice, and the regulation of social behavior. By focusing on these key areas, scholars can shed light on the mechanisms of legal governance and the dynamics of power and authority in ancient societies.

Furthermore, future research can explore the implications of ancient legal principles and practices for contemporary legal scholarship and practice. By drawing parallels between ancient and modern legal systems, scholars can identify enduring themes and values that continue to shape the administration of justice in the modern world. Moreover, by critically examining the ethical implications of ancient legal norms and principles, scholars can contribute to ongoing debates about justice, morality, and human rights in contemporary society.

Made in United States
Orlando, FL
03 June 2024